When Wisdom Speaks, Knowledge Listens

When Wisdom Speaks, Knowledge Listens

Waticia Floyd McDonald

XULON PRESS

Xulon Press
2301 Lucien Way #415
Maitland, FL 32751
407.339.4217
www.xulonpress.com

© 2020 by Waticia Floyd McDonald

All rights reserved solely by the author. The author guarantees all contents are original and do not infringe upon the legal rights of any other person or work. No part of this book may be reproduced in any form without the permission of the author. The views expressed in this book are not necessarily those of the publisher.

Unless otherwise indicated, Scripture quotations taken from the King James Version (KJV) – *public domain.*

Scripture quotations taken from the English Standard Version (ESV). Copyright © 2001 by Crossway, a publishing ministry of Good News Publishers. Used by permission. All rights reserved.

Scripture quotations taken from the New English Translation (NET Bible). Copyright ©1996-2006 by Biblical Studies Press, L.L.C. Used by permission. All rights reserved.

Paperback ISBN-13: 978-1-6322-1290-0

Ebook ISBN-13: 978-1-6322-1291-7

Acknowledgements

I am full of gratitude for all the guidance, mentorship, and wisdom from the people in my life. First, I thank The Holy Spirit. He was my helper and sustainer that assisted me in getting through the long nights and early mornings of writing. Secondly, I would like to thank my beloved husband, Benjamin T. McDonald, II for his push, prayer, and protection. He is my number one fan and would not allow me to operate in anything but the spirit of excellence. Thank God for both my parents, the late honorable, Bishop E. Floyd, Jr. and Prophetess Armatha Best Floyd—the very epitome of what a Christian Family was ordained to be. I thank my best friend and prayer partner, my sister, Otavia L. Floyd, and my big brother, Lawrence Floyd for always pushing me into greatness! I also would like to thank the host of Prophets, Elders, and my ancestors that are too numerous to list for their prophecy of this movement in ministry. I appreciate Apostle Titus Wesley and Dr. Tangula Diggs for your guidance and mentorship. Mr. Bernard Williams, thank you for bringing my vision to life and refusing to take no for an answer. Additionally, I am grateful to my photographer, Ms. Ashmear Livingston CEO of Love's Photography, my circle of prayer warriors for your encouragement to not let this assignment die. Thank my church family for praying and supporting me during this birthing process. This ministry is born! There is nothing that our God cannot do! This is just the beginning of an open-door season of dimensions to come.

Introduction

When Wisdom Speaks, Knowledge Listens is an unconventional Devotional Booklet that was inspired by my Father, the late honorable Bishop E. Floyd, Jr. He was the epitome of inspiration for his family, friends, and all who were blessed to be in his presence. He was passionate about the Gospel of Jesus Christ and God's people.

For me, wisdom was my father and mother. I have come to understand that everyone needs those small whispers of wisdom in their ears from time to time. My mother, who continues to push me today, embodies wisdom, strength, and courage. After my father left his earthly vessel to be with the Lord, a piece of my heart was taken as well. I was not empty by any means because he made certain that I was full of his wisdom before he made his departure. Although, he is not with us physically, I can still hear those small whispers at times when making even the smallest or major decisions. I grew up in the home of a Pastor and Bishop who were strict but compassionate simultaneously. He, along with my mom, would always say the wisest, comical, influential phrases that were filled with declarations that would unleash God's power. I'm compelled to share these phrases with the world in hopes that it will encourage and direct someone to God.

Congratulations, When Wisdom Speaks, Knowledge Listens found you! Yet, this book will not leave you in the same emotional or spiritual state. God will fill your heart with His presence and with His grace. To Him be the Glory for all that He is about to do for you. My prayer is that each week will increase your capacity for God, deepen your relationship with Him and you will follow His instructions. Blessings and Favor!

Life's journey begins now. Let us get started.

Week 1:

"Praise the Lord Everybody!"

The command, "Praise the Lord" is what all of creation was created to do. The wind shall praise God, when it blows, the trees praise God when it sways, the rivers praise God when it flows, the animals praise God when they make the sound they were created to make.

It is the expression of adoration or approval. We praise the Lord for his works, his character, and his traits. Praise includes the acts of blessings, commending, honoring, thanking, celebrating, and rejoicing. So what does it really mean? It may depend on who you are asking as to its perception. Often times it has another perception as well. For instance, if you meet someone from church in town or anywhere, the phrase is used to "greet" people, by saying hello, hi or how are you doing? In past generations, they understood for both parties to say it back. On the other hand, in church it is a command as indicated in the above definition.

Psalm 117:1-2 {NIV} *Praise the Lord, all you nations; extol him, all you peoples. For great is his love toward us, and the faithfulness of the Lord endures forever. Praise ye the Lord.* Paul quotes this verse in Romans 15:8-13.

What does it mean to you and how will you apply it this week?

Week 2:

"You don't have to say anything, I know I scored."

Often there will be people in your life that admire you, want to be like you but will never tell you. In this life, you must be self-motivated. Move past waiting on folk to congratulate, validate, or celebrate you. Be your own encourager. For seven days, encourage yourself and stop waiting for someone else to do it. You are your biggest fan. Jot down or tell yourself something encouraging every day this week!

<u>1 Samuel 30:6</u> {NIV} *David was greatly distressed because the men were talking of stoning him; each one was bitter in spirit because of his sons and daughters. But David found strength in the LORD his God.*

What does it mean to you and how will you apply it this week?

Week 3:

Now, I know this is going to be a little "edgy."

Often, we are placed in uncomfortable situations where we must address specific solutions or situations that need our attention. The phrase applies to the leader in you that must think first and react last. When you must address an audience, a friend or relative that may take offense to everything someone does. This phrase is an "ice breaker" that introduces the way to inform the other party that you are about to tell them the truth, the whole truth and nothing but the truth, so help you God. In other words, you are asking them to take down their defenses as you ease your way into it. It will always be important that you think before you speak. You don't ever want to intentionally hurt someone's feelings. Sometimes the way the truth is delivered may cause confrontation.

Ephesians 4:25 {KJV} *Therefore each of you must put off falsehood and speak truthfully to your neighbor, for we are all members of one body.*

What does it mean to you and how will you apply it this week?

Week 4:

"Whatever you commit to, it's got to be in your Heart!"

What are you willing to commit to? What do you think your heart feels? Listen, you are the only one that can answer that question. We must be strategic in our thought process. We, as millennials, will sometime have ideas and dreams but lack the commitment to accomplish the mission. You may ask, how can it get in your heart. First, there are three gateways to your heart— your ears, mouth, and eyes. Make sure these three are on one accord. The three must agree on what is being transmitted into your heart. What are you hearing? What are you saying? What are you seeing? I encourage you to research and find scriptures this week that deal with the heart and read them orally.

Matthew 6:21{KJV} *"For where your treasure is, there your heart will be also."*

What does it mean to you and how will you apply it this week?

Week 5:

"That thing you are trying to hide is the very thing God wants to use for HIs Glory".

The glory of God's grace and mercy is greatly displayed when we use our weakness and failures for His glory. This generation is more transparent than generations before us. It can be a downfall if you let it. Testimonies of God's deliverance can help some or hinder a carnal mind. Before you share, use wisdom by asking for God's permission. Not every testimony is meant to be shared. Therefore, it is so important to have the spirit of discernment and a close relationship with God. Often, we divulge things with the wrong people, and they try to hold it against you. Not everyone has your best interest at heart. Some people cannot handle your weaknesses and instead of praying for you, they are preying on you. Ask God for spiritual discernment this week, to know what to share and what not to share during your testimony.

Proverbs 25:2{NIV} *"It is the glory of God to conceal a matter; to search out a matter is the glory of kings."*

What does it mean to you and how will you apply it this week?

Week 6:

"I am different, and I am OK with that."

If you really think about it, we are all different. God created us with <u>unique features</u>, personalities, and traits. It is our responsibility to embrace the differences and give thanks to God because He created you to do great things. The human race is made up of many different colors, shapes, and sizes. That is an awesome package. Someone else once said, "Don't be afraid of being different but you should be afraid of being the same as everyone else." You will never accomplish great things if you are the same as the world. Many times we have to be reminded that we do as God tells us and not what people want us to do. You do not live for material things but you live for Christ. Material things will be added unto you as you please God. You are the righteousness of God. Pleasing God and bringing fame to his name is our priority. How can you use your difference to glorify God this week?

Romans 12:6-8 {NLT} *In his grace, God has given us different gifts for doing certain things well. So if God has given you the ability to prophesy, speak out with as much faith as God has given you. If your gift is serving others, serve them well. If you are a teacher, teach well. If your gift is to encourage others, be encouraging. If it is giving, give generously. If God has given you leadership ability, take the responsibility seriously. And if you have a gift for showing kindness to others, do it gladly.*

What does it mean to you and how will you apply it this week?

Week 7:

"The most important place to be is in the WILL of GOD. Am I in His will?"

Figuring out where you are in the plan of God is often made harder than it truly is. Seeking the will of God can be obtained by praying and asking God what his purpose is for your life. Being in the will of God, divine will, or God's plan is the concept of God having a plan designed just for you. Praying and spending time with God is a very important part of finding out what God's will is for your life. Set aside a time during the day that you will only be in the presence of God. This way, you can hear from Him. God will speak to you when you seek Him. Try to eliminate any distractions this week. Keep your mind on searching for God's will for your life. When you pray, wait for Him to speak back to you. I promise he will speak back.

Romans 12:2 {KJV} *Do not be conformed to this world, but be transformed by the renewal of your mind, that by testing you may discern what is the will of God, what is good and acceptable and perfect.*

What does it mean to you and how will you apply it this week?

Week 8:

*If you don't like me for me,
you won't like me at all!*

Basically, this phrase mean, a person should not change for others to like them. We all have different personalities, outlooks, and opinions. Do not allow others to make you feel like you are not enough. You do not have to adjust for anyone else. Be the best version of yourself that you can be. Live for God and please Him only. Everything else will follow. Love God with all your heart, soul, mind, and strength. Love your neighbor as yourself. There is no commandment greater than love.

Psalms 139:14 {KJV} *"I will praise You, for I am fearfully and wonderfully made; Marvelous are Your works, and that my soul knows very well."*

What does it mean to you and how will you apply it this week?

Week 9:

"You have to learn to live your life God's way."

We are the Lord's and we were purchased with his blood. Our goal is to make God famous by living our lives to bring God glory. You may ask, how can you live your life God's way. The deeper you grow in God, the deeper your relationship will become with him and the clearer his wishes develop for your life. Talk to God like he is your closest friend this week. Become intimate with your words to get his attention. God wants relationship from you not just weekend visits on Sunday. Ask God what you can do to bring him glory this week. Make this your daily goal and be accountable to someone if you fall short. When you die in Christ, you will rise with Christ!

Romans 14:8 {ESV} *For if we live, we live for the Lord, or if we die, we die for the Lord; therefore, whether we live or die, we are the Lord's.*

What does it mean to you and how will you apply it this week?

Week 10:

"When God says go, go on!"

Sometimes we fail at allowing God to lead and guide us because when he speaks, our flesh may not agree. We, as a generation, must understand that we are in warfare against ourselves every day. As a child of God, sometimes you will have to go into uncomfortable places. Sometimes you may have to get out of your comfort zone. Some people are afraid of hospitals, prisons, or even rest homes. What if these were the places God wanted you to go for ministry? God could be sending you to the most terrible neighborhoods to pray, and because all you see is danger, you refuse. This week ask God to lead you into places that are not within your comfort zone. Do something you have never done. Watch God stretch your faith and grow your mind. God will never leave you, nor will He forsake you.

John 16:13 {ESV} *When the Spirit of truth comes, he will guide you into all the truth, for he will not speak on his own authority, but whatever he hears he will speak, and he will declare to you the things that are to come.*

What does it mean to you and how will you apply it this week?

Week 11:

"Forget what's been done; it came to past. (Let go of it)"

We make mistakes and we learn from them. This week, forgive yourself. My father use to teach us that there are three forgiving techniques that will change your life forever: ask God to forgive you, forgive others, and forgive yourself. There are so many scriptures in the Bible that incorporate the phrase, "And it came to pass." Any situation that happened in your past came to pass. God is counting on us not to remember our past because he has forgotten it. God is so graceful and merciful that he renews his grace for us every day by giving us new mercies. Let go and let God fight your battles this week. We are all battling something that we need to simply let go. Hurt, Stress, Disappointment, Unforgiveness, etc. Let it go this week! This could be your day for FREEDOM!

Philippians 3:13-14 {KJV} *Brethren, I count not myself to have apprehended: but this one thing I do, forgetting those things which are behind, and reaching forth unto those things which are before, I press toward the mark for the prize of the high calling of God in Christ Jesus.*

What does it mean to you and how will you apply it this week?

Week 12:

"Watch people that have a lot of friends. This walk gets lonely sometimes."

There is no denying that often times these roads of suffering are incredibly <u>lonely</u>. Yes, it is true that there is nothing new under the sun (Ecclesiastes 1:9), and often there are more people who can relate to our suffering than we realize. Nevertheless, it does not change the fact that these roads are often still lonely. When you take a stand against the enemy, just know that you are not by yourself although it feels like you are. God is with you during your most difficult times. What you sacrifice in secret, God will reward you openly. I remember the days where I would get upset when I saw people receiving blessings that I knew were not producing valuable fruit. The Bible lets us know that we should not judge people, but we can judge the fruit they bare. Keep pressing into the things of God and be not weary in well doing this week. Watch your company and choose wisely who you interact with. This is perhaps a declaration that you can take with you the entire year.

<u>1 Corinthians 15:33</u>{AMP}*"Do not be deceived: "Bad company ruins good morals."*

What does it mean to you and how will you apply it this week?

Week 13:

"Are you praying ENOUGH?"

My father, Bishop E. Floyd Jr, Pastor of the United Pentecostal Churches of Christ would often ask people at church, "Are you praying enough?" I use to ponder over that phrase because it was evident that I wasn't praying enough. The results I desired from God were not manifesting. God longs for us to have a relationship with Him that is uninterrupted by our own desires and distractions. He desires for us to pray and give thanks in all seasons of our life. There is a song I use to sing, "Don't wait until midnight." This song asks that people not wait until they go through a crisis before they call out to God for help and direction. We should pray during the peaceful seasons as well as the stormy seasons of our life. This week decide that you will pray even more than you did before. In Daniel 6:10, Daniel had a custom of praying three times a day. God invites people to draw close to him in prayer. This week give thanks unto the Father evermore. Pray more than Daniel this week! Increase your time and watch God increase you!

1 Thessalonians 5:16-18 {AMP} *Rejoice evermore. Pray without ceasing. In everything give thanks, for this is the will of God in Christ Jesus concerning you.*

What does it mean to you and how will you apply it this week?

Week 14:

"Are you bringing Joy to the World or Silent Night?"

This is a phrase my mother, Prophetess Armatha Best Floyd, often says at times. It could be perceived in two ways. First, if your conversation lacks good news and tidings, you should be watchful and not wasteful with your words. Words have power and we should be careful with them. You can decree and declare things over your life in mere talk. Secondly, you could be like "Silent Night." Yes, I know the title is well known because it is a Christmas song, but its meaning is far from it. If you are silent, you choose to forfeit your opportunities to unlock doors, unleash blessings and break through into your life. My mother does not sugarcoat foolishness. Sometimes the best response is no response at all. In contrast her response is, "Silent Night."

God created the world with words and His power. Think about what you can create this week with His power and your words. Watch your words carefully and ensure they are bringing joy to the world. Encourage someone with your words and spread good news.

Luke 2:10-11{NIV} *"Don't be afraid," he said. "I bring you good news that will bring great JOY to all people. The Savior – yes, the Messiah, the Lord – has been born today in Bethlehem, the city of David!*

What does it mean to you and how will you apply it this week?

Week 15

"Sing your favorite song this week!"

Find a song that speaks to your spirit and invites you into the presence of God. There may be more than one. Songs that wake up your sleeping spirit. Music goes back over 40,000 years ago and will always be present. Even if you do not think you can sing, SING!!! Sing in the shower, sing your song all week and allow God to speak to your spirit through a song.

Psalm 95:1-2 {ESV} *Oh come, let us sing to the Lord; let us make a joyful noise to the rock of our salvation! Let us come into his presence with thanksgiving; let us make a joyful noise to him with songs of praise!*

What does it mean to you and how will you apply it this week?

Week 16:

"Women pray for your husband. Men pray for your wife. If you are not married, and desire to be, continue to seek God so that your husband/wife will find you. Thank God in advance by praying for them beforehand."

It is most important for wives to cover your husband and hold him up in prayer. He needs you to support him and bring peace to his mind and spirit. When a husband and wife decide to become one, what happens in his or her life also happens in yours. You are to build together. It is a house and with brick by brick you accomplish the goal in building an empire. Make sure that you are in the right season of your life. If you are not married, before God will allow you to find the right one that fits your mind, body, and soul. Pray and be sure to make your request known. Do it God's way. His ways are so much higher than yours, and He knows exactly what He is doing. May God's peace and His will be released into your relationship this week. Speak it in advance!

Proverbs 18:22 {NIV} *He who finds a wife finds what is good and receives FAVOR from the Lord.*

What does it mean to you and how will you apply it this week?

Week 17:

"It is open door season for me and those connected to me!"

Jesus, as the truth, offers an unbiased assessment of the Church at Philadelphia. Jesus opens doors that no man can shut and closes doors that no man can open. He opened a door of opportunity in front of the church. He describes the church as having little power but used that power to His effect. When we remain loyal and obey his words, we reap the benefits and those who are connected to us reap also. That is why in earlier weeks during this booklet, you were instructed to watch your company. Not only does this matter when God is passing out blessings, but it matters that you do not connect with someone who will cause you to become defeated. Pray for your entire family, children, and friends this week. When God blesses you and opens doors for you, do not walk through them alone, but take them with you.

Revelation 3:8 {ESV} *I know your works. Behold, I have set before you an open door, which no one is able to shut. I know that you have but little power, and yet you have kept my word and have not denied my name.*

What does it mean to you and how will you apply it this week?

Week 18:

"I'm going to pray that Kingdom down!"

My mom, Prophetess Armatha Floyd, is a prayer warrior and doesn't mind letting the world know it. Often, we are faced with kingdoms that God did not build. These kingdoms are created by satanic forces, either because of our disobedience or our failure to seek the will of God. We end up in situations that we must pray our way out of. With a solid prayer life, we become strong in the spirit. We must add fasting to our spiritual lifestyle in order for us to change. Fasting and praying changes you. Some may not agree but fasting and praying also changes your situation as well. God is a rewarder to those who diligently seek him. Believe God this week. Trust Him. The kingdoms that God did not build, are coming down in Jesus's name. Go in and pray that kingdom down! You are a Kingdom citizen and you have rights to the throne! Set aside your fasting and prayer time this week and get ready for your testimony!

Matthew 17:21{KJV} *Howbeit this kind goeth not out but by prayer and fasting.*

What does it mean to you and how will you apply it this week?

Week 19:

"Something's got a hold on me!" (The Holy Spirit)

This phrase is normally stated when the Holy Spirit takes over your life and changes your perspective of the situations you face, circumstances you're in and how you respond to them. As a Christian, no one ever said you would be exempt from having to go through challenges. Often as a child of God, you have to endure more because it's a daily war between God and Satan. Satan is fighting for your soul every day and wants you to give in to the temptations you are faced with. The devil does not come up with new ideas but often finds new tactics to hit us with the same objectives in mind. Once you learn how to fight back in the spirit, you will have a greater hold on the things of God and be more prepared to retaliate. Something's got a hold of me and it makes me love my enemies. It makes me want to pray when my flesh does not want to pray. The Holy Spirit is what has this hold on me. I pray it never lets me go. This week seek more of God's Holy Spirit. Allow it be your teacher. Let it be your guide into the deeper things of God. The Holy Spirit is referred to as "He". Truly, He is the Creator, Spirit. He is present before the creation of the universe and through His power everything was made in Jesus Christ, by God the Father. The Holy Spirit is understood to be one of the three in the Trinity. The Father, Son, and the Holy Spirit, all in one Godhead. Ask God this week, "What can I do to please you today?"

Romans 8:26 {ESV} *Likewise the Spirit helps us in our weakness. For we do not know what to pray for as we ought, but the Spirit himself intercedes for us with groanings too deep for words.*

What does it mean to you and how will you apply it this week?

Week 20:

"You cannot control the actions of other people, but you can control how you react."

God has called us to be his people and in the last days people will be lovers of themselves just as the scripture below states. This is your week of purpose. Make a difference by allowing God to help you control your actions even when people around you seem to have a different aspect or perception towards the purpose that you share. We are all surrounded by people who are possibly unholy, negative, spiteful, conceited, arrogant, deceitful, and full of pride but we must control how we react to them. We must understand that we cannot control their actions. Often it makes us upset. We cannot control the lifestyles of others that we must be around; therefore, we must pray for them and carry on in Jesus' name. Make it your priority to change your reaction this week!

2 Timothy 3:1-6 {ESV} *But understand this, that in the last days there will come times of difficulty. For people will be lovers of self, lovers of money, proud, arrogant, abusive, disobedient to their parents, ungrateful, unholy, heartless, unappeasable, slanderous, without self-control, brutal, not loving good, treacherous, reckless, swollen with conceit, lovers of pleasure rather than lovers of God, having the appearance of godliness, but denying its power. Avoid such people.*

What does it mean to you and how will you apply it this week?

Week 21:

"God is in control of my situation and I declare VICTORY this week!"

We serve a God that makes things happen with His mouth. Declare victory and it shall be yours. Whatever you are going after this week, remember God has promised you an expected end, which is Victory. Do not look back but continue to press forward into the things of God. Even in your weaknesses, God is your strength. He has already given you the win. You are on Victory's side. This will be a week of multiple Victories. You have been praying and fasting and the day has arrived that your prayers will be answered. God will show himself mightily and strong in your life. Look for the supernatural to take place. Your loss is a WIN when you have positioned yourself in the will of God. Watch God work for you this week. It is going to be big. Decree and declare this all week.

Deuteronomy 20:4 {ESV} *For the Lord your God is he who goes with you to fight for you against your enemies, to give you the victory.*

What does it mean to you and how will you apply it this week?

Week 22:

"This week will line up with GOD's plan for my life!"

Have you ever wanted to take a different path than what God wants for you? I can identify with that. Before consulting God, I thought, I knew what I wanted in life and what direction I wanted to take. Sometimes, what we want, can be good, but is it God. We could be blessed by choosing a career, a school to attend, etc. but when we line up with what God wants for our life, the favor of God overwhelms us. Ask God if your life is aligned with his plans. Every week, we want the Holy Spirit to lead us. Let us stay focused, because sometimes we drift too far away from God to hear His words. I often say, "Lord I want to be so close to you, that I hear your thoughts as well as your words." How close are you to God? Get closer this week.

John 14:20 {ESV} *In that day you will know that I am in my Father, and you in me, and I in you.*

What does it mean to you and how will you apply it this week?

Week 23:

"It's time to Repent!"

Let this be a week of repentance. Find yourself repenting for everything that's in you that God did not ordain in your character. Seek to build upon the characteristic of Jesus, who is our example. Repent daily. There are 52 weeks in the year, but you should repent daily for things that you are unaware of that you may have said, done, or thought. You do not want to be caught in suffering for a lack of knowledge. REPENT, as it is never too late or too early to do so. Ask God to help you turn away from anything that is not pleasing to Him or brings glory to His name! There are no super stars within the body of Christ. There is only God. We are all in the body of Christ and operate utilizing our own functionality. When you operate outside of your purposed function, you malfunction. Therefore, it is so important to seek the will of God. This week repent and keep a pure heart. Only the pure in heart will see God!

<u>2 Peter 3:9</u> {ESV} *The Lord is not slow to fulfill his promise as some count slowness, but is patient toward you, not wishing that any should perish, but that all should reach repentance.*

What does it mean to you and how will you apply it this week?

Week 24:

"The questions you can't answer is God's way of inviting you to seek Him."

The only one that knows everything is GOD. Although there are people who think they know more than Him, they are sadly mistaken. Our God is all knowing, omnipresent and omniscient. <u>Psalm 139:7-12</u> {ESV} *Where shall I go from your Spirit? Or where shall I flee from your presence? If I ascend to heaven, you are there! If I make my bed in Sheol, you are there! If I take the wings of the morning and dwell in the uttermost parts of the sea, even there your hand shall lead me, and your right hand shall hold me. If I say, "Surely the darkness shall cover me, and the light about me be night," even the darkness is not dark to you; the night is bright as the day, for darkness is as light with you."* Ask God to enlighten you this week and give you new strategies that will bring him Glory. Believe that when you seek God for His glory, he will favor you in areas that you would never think of. Encourage yourself to dig deeper into the things of God. You will never get all of Him. Allow His Holy Spirit to help you uncover ideas that you have bottled up. You are gifted and God knew it first. Start this week by seeking God for unanswered questions so that you can receive a strategic response that will get you going in the right direction. It is never too late. There is something great waiting on you and it shall be blessed.

<u>Ecclesiastes 1:9</u> {ESV} *What has been is what will be, and what has been done is what will be done, and there is nothing new under the sun.*

What does it mean to you and how will you apply it this week?

Week 25:

"When you pray, speak from a place of submission."

God is our ultimate guide and leader. Pastors have been set aside to lead and guide us. I've been a secondary leader for years. I'm a PK (Pastor's Kid). This is not always what it appears to be in the public eye. Pastors have so much to endure from people who say they love them and will serve with submission. This week ask God what you can do to help your Pastor's load become easier. It is your job to have the heart of your Pastor. Where there is no vision the people perish. Serve with gratitude, grace, submission and with servanthood. When you do not agree with your Pastor or anyone for that fact that has been placed in a position of authority over you, submit with grace. Oftentimes you may not understand their decisions concerning matters, submit. A pastor should be led by God and you should trust their decisions even if you don't always understand them. However, your submitted to someone else in authority, do what is right according to the Word of God. Not everyone in authority is led by God. When you pray, you will be led to a place of submission with the help of God. By doing this, you submit your wants to His will. Please God by glorifying Him in all that you do.

Hebrews 13:17 {ESV} *Obey your leaders and submit to them, for they are keeping watch over your souls, as those who will have to give an account. Let them do this with joy and not with groaning, for that would be of no advantage to you.*

What does it mean to you and how will you apply it this week?

Week 26:

"Ask God to disrupt your normalcy."

Often times we become complacent because we are comfortable in that place. We feel like its God's will. There may be something you've dealt with for years and it looks good, feels good, but it isn't good for you. So what, you've done it for years, but God says it's time you switch it up. Ask God for new ideas, ask God for strategic moves that will open up something different in your life. Change should be welcomed. Most people don't like change. Who wants to do things the same way, year in and year out? Wake up Zion! Let's start this week by seeking God for a change in the way you approach things, situations or just whatever area of your life that needs a little tweaking. God will use this change to His advantage this week. Are you ready for change!! Say this, "Holy Spirit prepare me this week for a supernatural change! I am ready to obey!"

Luke 6:46 {ESV} *Why do you call me 'Lord, Lord,' and not do what I tell you?*

What does it mean to you and how will you apply it this week?

Week 27:

"Find you some friends who love you too much to let you go to hell!"

My father and mother always told me, "Find friends who will hold you accountable for the wrong that you do. Find you friends that won't go along with everything you do that is not godly." You need people who will call you out and do it with the right spirit. Of course, they cannot rebuke you if they are doing the same thing you are doing. That would be like the blind leading the blind! Therefore, you cannot be yoked with people who do not believe like you. ESV, Psalms 14:1, "The fool says in his heart, "There is no God." They are corrupt, they do abominable deeds; there is none who does good." I want friends that can partner with me in prayer, fasting and devotion to God. For this week, make sure you partner up with a friend that will not allow you to be *hell* bound!

This week, you are challenged to find you a friend who does not want you to go to *hell*. The love and concern should be mutual because you should not want your friend to go to *hell* as well. If you are wondering what that means, let me enlighten you. It is, you are calling sin what it is, sin! Cover them in prayer but not in their wrongdoings. Some friends are not open to constructive criticism; however, that is not the case with true friends. Seek out consistent and loyal friends. If you are a friend, be a friend indeed.

Proverbs 18:24 {ESV} *A man of many companions may come to ruin, but there is a friend who sticks closer than a brother.*

What does it mean to you and how will you apply it this week?

Week 28:

My parents always taught me, "Don't put all your eggs in one basket."

This advice means we should not concentrate all our efforts into one resource but have multiple resources. We do this so that we are not at risk of losing everything all at once. Find yourself striving to have at least seven to eight different streams of income, investments, or resource entries.

Ecclesiastes 11:2 {NIV} *Invest in seven ventures, yes in eight; you do not know what disaster may come upon the land.*

What does it mean to you and how will you apply it this week?

Week 29

"Stand up for something or fall for anything!"

In life, we all will be faced with difficult decisions or circumstances. When we are approached with peer pressure, we should never jeopardize our integrity, values, and morals that have been instilled in us. Having a firm foundation will keep you honest so you do not stray. We all have a belief in something. Stand firm on it, build on it, and follow through with it. Stand up for what is right, even if you are the only one standing. It is okay to be different. When you do what's right, it will never go unnoticed. God is a rewarder to those who diligently seek after Him. Continue in the faith because someone's life depends on it. Do not be easily influenced with every wind of direction. This week's challenge is to always do what is right unto God.

Colossians 1:23{NIV} *"If you continue in your faith, established and firm, and do not move from the hope held out in the gospel. This is the gospel that you heard and that has been proclaimed to every creature under heaven, and of which I, Paul, have become a servant."*

What does it mean to you and how will you apply it this week?

Week 30:

"My fruit still remains, even in a pandemic!"

This just happens to be during the 2020 Worldwide Pandemic due to Covid-19. The world stood still and we were encouraged to stay indoors. The CDC (Center for Disease Control) advised everyone to remain home, not to travel, or to be in large crowds of people. This was the time where the Lord spoke to my Mother about producing fruit in a pandemic. Be fruitful in everything you do! You may ask, what is being fruitful. It is having the ability to produce something. As a Christian, we must be good stewards so that we can successfully produce. We must remain fruitful even when our regular routine has been interrupted. Separation makes the heart grow. Ask yourself, which direction are you growing in and from what are you growing. This is a time that we must be fruitful with our time, talents, and money. These are instances in which the enemy will try and attempt to distract you from producing. This is literally wisdom speaking to a generation and if you have knowledge, you will listen. I challenge you to spend less time on social media and be more productive with your time. I challenge you to embrace your God given talents. Ask God to help you become strategic with it, so that you may glorify his name. Lastly, I challenge you to invest your money wisely. Seek out an accountant who can help you. Work with someone to increase your credit score, pay off some smaller bills. Overall, be a good steward and bear fruit!

John 15:16 {NIV} *You did not choose me, but I chose you and appointed you so that you might go and bear fruit—fruit that will last—and so that whatever you ask in my name the Father will give you.*

What does it mean to you and how will you apply it this week?

Week 31:

"That demon may be tamed but it's not out!"

Many times, people will operate in the flesh and say it is God. Ask God for spiritual discernment so that you are not led astray. Sometimes people are not fully delivered from the same thing they are teaching or preaching. Find yourself practicing what you preach, by living what you preach. If you are a singer, live what you sing. If you are a teacher, live what you teach. The best way to tell someone about Christ is to show them with your life. Be the person you want others to be. Be the first partaker of God's deliverance, so that you can genuinely lead someone out of the same thing you struggled with. This week seek God in every area of your life that needs deliverance and expect God to do it. You shall have a testimony this week! Whatever it is, give it to God. We all have one thing or some things that need the hand of God. This week you will get free and stay free! Rejoice for your Healing!

<u>1 John 4:1</u> {ESV} *"Beloved, do not believe every spirit, but test the spirits to see whether they are from God, for many false prophets have gone out into the world."*

What does it mean to you and how will you apply it this week?

Week 32:

"It is well with my soul!"

The hymn "It Is Well with My Soul" expresses the joy of a Christian poet over the glad consciousness of a saving relationship with Jesus Christ. Assurance of salvation is possible for every believer (1 John 5:13). Assurance makes peace of mind and heart possible. It also makes effective service possible. In the Bible, the Fruit of the Spirit is peace. This is a song that has many different versions. It begins with the verse, "When peace like a river." It compares the peace of God to a river that flows freely. There are no distractions, hindrances, blocks, or detours to the flow of a river. In Romans 5:1, Paul explains how we were in the past. We were enmity with God because of our sin, but when Christ came, it gave us an opportunity to have God's peace. In this sense, God can give you a peace that surpasses all understanding. You could be going through your greatest battle, your greatest disappointment but God's peace has a way of emerging you into a place of comfort and healing. It is not what you go through but it is how you go through it. Your perception of the battle can either give you strength to win or fear to fail. This week go through with God's peace and with His Faith and know that it is well with your soul!

Psalm 62:1 {NIV} *"Truly my soul finds rest in God; my salvation comes from him."*

What does it mean to you and how will you apply it this week?

Week 33:

"Worry is a down payment for problems."

We all worry. Pray to God to remove your worry and anxiety. We feel insecure on the job, in school from peer pressure, fear for our kids' future, concerns about our health and maybe in our ability to pay for our healthcare, not to mention, our mortgage, car payments and the list goes on. Some people result to a host of solutions like meditation, psychotherapy, anti-anxiety medications, etc. The most important source of support is our hope in the Word of God, The Holy Bible. The scriptures are our lifelines that speak to every problem that we go through in life. Some may not know it, but scriptures are therapeutic. Search the scriptures this week for all your needs and read it daily. Allow God to pick the words off the paper and apply them to your situation. There is healing for your sorrow and healing for your soul.

Philippians 4:6-7{ NKJV} *"Be anxious for nothing, but in everything by prayer and supplication, with thanksgiving let your request be made known to God; and the peace of God which surpasses all understanding, will guard your hearts and minds through Christ Jesus."*

What does it mean to you and how will you apply it this week?

Week 34:

"Give your problems to God and leave them there. Get some rest because God is up all night long."

Since last week you were instructed not to worry unless you want welcome problems. This week you are instructed to release your problems into the hands of God and leave them there. Often my Father would sing the song by the Canton Spirituals, "Doctor Jesus said he would make everything alright." If you are going to worry, do not pray; and if you pray, do not worry. Our God is the Great Counselor. Let go and let God do it. You must realize that you are human and do not have to control everything. Admit that you do not have all the answers and need to take a moment to regroup. Take a deep breath and pray that God gives you the wisdom to hear what He is saying. Realize you are human, and somethings will be out of your control. No matter how awesome and capable you are, God is still the answer to all of your problems.

Proverbs 12:25 {ESV} *Anxiety in a man's heart weighs him down, but a good word makes him glad.*

1 Peter 5:7 {NIV} *Cast all your anxiety on him because he cares for you.*

Philippians 4:6 {ESV} *Do not be anxious about anything, but in everything by prayer and supplication with thanksgiving let your requests be made known to God.*

What does it mean to you and how will you apply it this week?

Week 35:

"May the work I've done, speak for me."

Ordinarily, this is a phrase used after the passing of someone who lived a life of sacrifice unto God. A servant who does not worry about what people say but is convinced that his/her life expresses God's love, His power, and His grace. John 10:25 speaks about the works that we as His children do in our Father's name. The disciples bear witness of God through the healing of the sick, dispossessing devils, cleansing lepers, giving sight to the blind, causing the deaf to hear, the dumb to speak, the lame to walk, and raising the dead to life. They had no reason to doubt in their mind that God was with them; nor had they any reason to complain of him hiding himself from them or depriving them of the knowledge of him.

John 10:25 {KJV} *"Jesus answered them, I told you, and ye believed not: the works that I do in my Father's name, they bear witness of me."*

What does it mean to you and how will you apply it this week?

Week 36:

*"It's not about what I feel
but it's what I already know God can do.
If God doesn't heal me, He is still able"*

God is able! During your life there will be times when you feel like you are going under and not over. You feel like you are going through trials and tribulations by yourself or if it is too much to bear. We should not allow the enemy to convince us that God is not with us. Remember this, God is with you and He is mighty to save you. God is with you through all that you go through. Even when you are at your lowest point, God is with you though the good and the bad times. Know that God will always make the crooked paths straight for His children. There is nothing impossible for our God.

Zephaniah 3:17 {NIV} *The LORD your God is with you, he is mighty to save. He will take great delight in you, he will quiet you with his love, he will rejoice over you with...*

What does it mean to you and how will you apply it this week?

Week 37:

"If you do not walk in faith, run in faith, but whatever you do, don't get STUCK without Faith."

My father's first sermon topic was, "Be Faithful". Book: Revelations 2:10. NIV *"¹⁰Do not be afraid of what you are about to suffer. I tell you, the devil will put some of you in prison to test you, and you will suffer persecution for ten days. Be faithful, even to the point of death, and I will give you life as your victor's crown."*

Many times, life can hand you disappointments. Life gives you a no. Life gives you the unexpected and plans do not always go as expected. You must always believe, keep hoping, and keep dreaming for God has strategically placed you where you are in preparation for your destiny. Never get stuck because your life appears as if it is on pause. Someone is depending on you to succeed. May you have consistent faith in God to work His plan in you. Watch God favor you!

<u>James 2:26</u> {KJV} *For as the body without the spirit is dead, so faith without works is dead.*

What does it mean to you and how will you apply it this week?

Week 38:

"If you cannot forgive, forget going to Heaven sir or ma'am."

If you ever want to be forgiven, you must be quick to forgive others. Think of a time when you made a mistake and needed forgiveness. Whether it was big or small, you needed forgiveness. If you need forgiveness, learn to forgive yourself, which means that you do not continue to beat yourself up over past mistakes. Ask God to help guide you. The Holy Spirit is a helper. When you genuinely ask God for help to glorify Him, He will offer His assistance. Often, we do not always give others the forgiveness that we want from God. How quickly do we forget that when someone does something against us? Oftentimes, we are ready to cast them aside. If we want mercy, we must show mercy. Be quick to forgive people because the forgiveness is not for them, but the forgiveness is for you. It is freedom! You make room for God to fight for you. Do not lose energy this week by holding grudges against people. If needed, forgive without the apology you deserve. Ask the Holy Spirit to help you forgive those who trespassed against you. You can do it and you can do it well!

<u>Matthew 6:15</u> {KJV} *"But if ye forgive not men their trespasses, neither will your Father forgive your trespasses."*

What does it mean to you and how will you apply it this week?

Week 39:

"Question for this week. How long will you be halted between two opinions?"

This phrase was used a lot by my Father in one of his sermons. He started with a question that made you analyze yourself. How many of us are indecisive? This question simply means that you have not made a choice concerning your Christian walk with God. Honestly, some folk love God but are so quick to live for the devil. In other words, you cannot live for God and the Devil. You cannot walk in the light and in darkness. You must choose one or the other. Although we all sin, we are not all sinners. A sinner continues to sin and chooses to walk in darkness. Choose God in every area of your life this week. You will be faced with decisions this week that could either make or break your Christian walk. Make a choice to do better. This booklet found its way to you on purpose.

Joshua 24:15 {KJV} *And if it seem evil unto you to serve the LORD, choose you this day whom ye will serve; whether the gods which your fathers served that were on the other side of the flood, or the gods of the Amorites, in whose land **ye** dwell: but as for me and my house, we will serve the Lord.*

What does it mean to you and how will you apply it this week?

Week 40:

"Be authentic from the inside out."

Some may say that this generation is more concerned about what things appear to be on the outside rather than what they really are. What is your reality? Are the opinions of others more important than the opinion of God? This is a question that should matter to you. God knows the heart and the soul's intent. Looking like you have it all together when you are really broken inside is a recipe for disaster. God wants his children healthy and whole from the inside out. You cannot be mean and hateful on the inside and then expect people to love you because you put up a facade. Your truth will eventually surface for the world to see the real you. If there are unsolved issues, talk to someone that you trust. Pray this week for God's help. Search deep inside for what makes you act like you do positively or negatively. You do not want to look blessed when you are really stressed. You do not want to look well on your way to hell. You do not want to look delivered when you are really hindered. Ask the Holy Spirit to free you from the inside out. Your task this week is to find a scripture that speaks to the problem that you battle within. It could be low self-esteem, unforgiveness, brokenness, bitterness, etc.

<u>Hebrews 12:14</u> {KJV} *"Follow peace with all men, and holiness, without which no man shall see the Lord."*

What does it mean to you and how will you apply it this week?

Week 41:

"Face it, there is no sin getting into Heaven."

We were born into sin but we can be born again. The Lord Jesus is our Redeemer and He sacrificed His life so that we might live a life of freedom from sin. Once we accept Jesus as our personal Savior, we believe that Jesus died for our sins and those of this world. Revelation 21:4 explains that there will not be any problems or pain any longer when we get to Heaven. Jesus dying for our sins wiped away every tear from our eyes and death, mourning, or crying shall be no more. Sin causes pain and heaven is a pure place. Our goal destination should be Heaven. Remember, that you need to live so you can live again!

Revelation 21:27 {ESV} *But nothing unclean will ever enter it, nor anyone who does what is detestable or false, but only those who are written in the Lamb's book of life.*

What does it mean to you and how will you apply it this week?

Week 42:

"When you have made the decision to forgive, anticipate the enemy bringing it back to your memory. This is what you must do this week. Mark it, "RETURN to SENDER."

So, in Week 38 you affirmed you would forgive. Guess what? The enemy will not allow you to get by that easy. You must learn to continuously walk in forgiveness. You won the battle in the 38th week by forgiving, so now make a conscience decision to continue down this righteous path. Just to give you a heads up, sometimes forgiveness takes more than doing it once. Sometimes, you will have to keep reminding yourself when the thought comes back to try and haunt you. Take control of your thoughts by speaking out loud. Refuse to continue to go back and forth with the same feelings that hurt you in the past. Decree that you have been delivered this week.

Isaiah 54:17 {ESV} *No weapon that is fashioned against you shall succeed, and you shall confute every tongue that rises against you in judgment. This is the heritage of the servants of the Lord and their vindication from me, declares the Lord."*

What does it mean to you and how will you apply it this week?

Week 43:

*"Line up the matters of the heart,
soul and spirit which are inside.
After doing so, the outside will fall into place."*

The matters of the heart, soul, and spirit are all intertwined into your individual fabric. It is what makes you a total being. What matters to your heart? What matters have made their way into your soul? What matters have you allowed into your spirit? Can you live without them? These are all questions that you must ask yourself this week. Focus on your affections, emotions, and conscience. The Lord wants you to have a relationship with Him that you work on daily. We must ensure our heart, soul, and spirit are aligned with what God desires of us. Our affections evolve around what we allow in. Everyone is responsible for what they allow into their heart, soul and spirit. Speak to God this week and ask Him to help you guard these three from all evil. My prayer is that God sends a supernatural release your way this week. Nothing but love and positivity will flow from your heart, soul, and spirit.

Colossians 3:2 {KJV} *Set your affection on things above, not on things on the earth.*

What does it mean to you and how will you apply it this week?

Week 44:

"God has a way to take ALL your pain and transform it into Power."

Think of all the pain you have had to endure or face throughout your life. This week you need to expect God to surpass all of your expectations about what He can do through what you had to endure. First, know that there was a reason why you had to go through and survive. Had you gotten stuck in the pain, you would not have the testimony that God is a way maker. This week, your testimony will be that you have gone from pain to purpose. Everything you have gone through in your past paved the way to your divine destiny in Jesus the Christ name. Everyone has a trial that has brought tribulation but there is Power in it. You must believe that something new will be birthed out of you this year, better yet, this week. Make a declaration to aspire for greatness from something that caused pain but produced power. Had you not gone through it, how would you know your purpose? You are anointed to produce, so do not be ashamed but give God glory. Something different is about to happen for you! Glory shall be your portion for all your sufferings!

Romans 8:18 {KJV} *For I reckon that the sufferings of this present time are not worthy to be compared with the glory which shall be revealed in us.*

What does it mean to you and how will you apply it this week?

Week 45:

"Keep living, Life will "learn" (teach) you."

My father and mother would tell me this all the time, so now I get the chance to share it with someone else. Life is precious and we must appreciate every day the Lord sends. "Life" in this quote represents conditions, situations, relationships, and circumstances. Life happens to all of us and will teach us something. What will it teach you, is the question? How will you handle what it teaches you? Exhibit what you have been taught by letting it speak volumes about your strength, integrity, and values you have obtained from a positive influence in your life. Was it your parents, grandparents, other family members, classmates, co-workers, or friends? Take God with you during this life, because although we do not know what our life will take us through, God does. He knows what we will face and what we will become. Do not allow life to get you down but stay focused and pray that the hand of God remains on your life.

Jeremiah 29:11 {KJV} *For I know the thoughts that I think toward you, saith the LORD, thoughts of peace, and not of evil, to give you an expected end.*

What does it mean to you and how will you apply it this week?

Week 46:

"You were designed to prosper and be in good health."

You were manufactured by God Almighty to function properly. Do not live beneath your means. You deserve the absolute best out of life. If you feel like you are just getting by, do something about it. Are you physically and spiritually in shape? If not, start this week. Do your research and find a physical health physician or training tool that will assist you on a healthier lifestyle change. Change your eating habits, proportions that you consume. Drink more water. Find a suitable exercise that will impact your body's definition. Since you are already taking this 52 Week journey reading, *When Wisdom Speaks, Knowledge Listens,* you have already taken the initiative to getting your spiritual lifestyle in order. Add this week's declaration to every week for the rest of your life or until you have reached your lifestyle's goals. It is going to take focus and determination. Let us be consistent and strategic with what we put into our mouth and our hearts this week!

3 John 1:2 {KJV} *Beloved, I wish above all things that thou mayest prosper and be in health, even as thy soul prospereth."*

What does it mean to you and how will you apply it this week?

Week 47:

"Don't ever feel overlooked because everyone is somebody but it's up to you to know exactly who you are."

Not knowing who you are can be extremely dangerous. You could be easily influenced in your decisions that are not in your best interest. Peer pressure is something every human being has faced. You must not underestimate the power you possess. Once you fall in love with God, allow His Holy Spirit to take precedence over everything in your life. Make Him ruler and King in every area of your life. Seek God's will for your life and what you have been purposed to do. You are important to God and you fit into his plan like a missing puzzle piece if you are out of His perfect will. Others will be intimidated when you know who you are in God, verses wondering through life trying to find your way. The key to finding out who you are is simple. Ask God to reveal it to you through His Word. Read His words in the "Holy Bible." Make sure your social circle is in the will of God. Be sure they are walking in Christ and seeking His will. Congratulate and be genuinely happy for others in their season of breakthrough. You will reap if you faint not. In some situations, God will let you be overlooked for a season because He is hiding you for His purpose. Wait patiently on the Lord. Your day will come!

John 11:25 {KJV} *Jesus said unto her, I am the resurrection, and the life: he that believeth in me, though he were dead, yet shall he live:*

What does it mean to you and how will you apply it this week?

Week 48:

"Remain teachable and reachable in order to retain a spirit of humility for a continuous learner."

Never become so arrogate that you think you can live without a mentor. Find a mentor that you can be accountable to, that you can talk to without judgement. However, allow them to judge what you are producing whether positive or negative. Let them feel comfortable sharing their wisdom with you. Always operate in humility so that you can reach others in life. No matter how much education you have received, what position you have obtained, remain humble. You must serve to be served. You must honor someone who has influenced your decisions in life, for example a pastor or mentor. Submit to this person like a father. However, if not a father, a mother, if not a sister, a brother, if not a family member, a friend, submit. There should be someone you can honor! Make sure you can honor someone of positive influence in your life. You will never obtain what you fail to honor! Pray to God for help in this area of your life. You are a leader, but you must follow first. Become one of God's disciples and then you will make disciples of men in God's honor! This week promise God that you will remain genuinely humble for the destiny He has for you!

1 Corinthians 4:15{KJV} *"For though ye have ten thousand instructors in Christ yet have ye not many fathers: for in Christ Jesus I have begotten you through the gospel."*

What does it mean to you and how will you apply it this week?

Week 49:

"Be a good steward. There is a difference between being busy and being productive"

If there is one thing you should do this week, it is to use your time wisely. Time is of the essence and if you know how valuable it is, you will not waste it unproductively. There are 24 hours in a day. Have you ever been so busy and wished there were more hours in the day? On the other hand, you are not as productive time tends to stand still. There is a difference in being busy and being productive. You could be busy being unproductive. If you are a good steward, you manage your time, finances, and relationships with productivity and God influence. Notice I did not say good influence. Just because it's good influence does not necessarily mean its God. The enemy (Satan) uses our time, finances, and relationships to cause us to either fail or succeed at life. God must be consulted first before you start or end your projects, investments, or interactions. Invest in your time, finances, and relationships so that you can have a residual income in those areas. If they are one-sided, they will fail. Finances where you are always investing and never receiving interest or income are wasteful. Relationships that you are always building without someone building you, are wasteful. This week steward these areas with the help of the Holy Spirit. You must give some and then you must receive in return. The process continues consistently in a pattern that is healthy for your life. Otherwise, you become unproductive, unwise, and unable to flourish in the grace of God concerning these things.

<u>1 Peter 4:10</u> {KJV} *As every man hath received the gift, even so minister the same one to another, as good stewards of the manifold grace of God.*

What does it mean to you and how will you apply it this week?

Week 50:

"Learn to be a blessing to people without telling everyone."

We should all have Godly hearts to serve and share with people who are less fortunate. The poor will always be amongst us. You can be blessed to be the one who can bless others. Blessing people does not have to always be tangible. You can be present in the lives of people that just need a listening ear—the elderly, the sick, the less fortunate, etc. When you are a help to these sisters and brothers who are in need, do not always live to tell others about what you have done for them. It is not for you to spread that you have helped the less fortunate. Let the good news spread through the mouth of others. Your life should be a testimony that God is glorified. There will be times that you will give God glory because you were able to give; however, God knows the intent of your heart and your objective for giving. Do not give for show or to be glorified in your own pride or selfishness. Some folk only give to post on social media outlets, newspapers, radio, television, and other means of communications, so the world may see or hear. Can I enlighten you? You have your reward if your motives are not pure.

Matthew 6:1-13 *{KJV} "Take heed that ye do not your alms before men, to be seen of them: otherwise ye have no reward of your Father which is in heaven. Therefore when thou doest thine alms, do not sound a trumpet before thee, as the hypocrites do in the synagogues and in the streets, that they may have glory of men. Verily I say unto you, they have their reward. But when thou doest alms, let not thy left hand know what thy right hand doeth: That thine alms may be in secret: and thy Father which seeth in secret himself shall reward thee openly. And when thou prayest, thou shalt* *not be as the hypocrites are: for they love to pray standing in the synagogues and in the corners of the streets, that they may be seen of men. Verily I say unto you, they have their reward. But thou, when thou prayest, enter into thy closet, and when thou hast shut thy door, pray to thy Father which is in secret; and thy Father which seeth in secret shall reward thee openly. But when ye pray, use not vain repetitions, as the heathen do: for they think that they shall be heard for their much speaking. Be not ye therefore like unto them: for your Father knoweth what things ye have need of, before ye ask him After this manner therefore pray ye: Our Father which art in heaven, Hallowed be thy name. Thy kingdom come, Thy will be done in earth, as it is in heaven. Give us this day our daily bread. And forgive us our debts, as we forgive our debtors. And lead us not into temptation but deliver us from evil: For thine is the kingdom, and the power, and the glory, forever. Amen."*

What does it mean to you and how will you apply it this week?

Week 51

"Make UP your mind and keep it there!"

The mind has so much control as to rather you succeed or fail at anything. Do you ever wonder why you must make UP your mind? Make sure that when you make UP your mind that the decision that you conclude is above and not beneath. Make sure that your mind is clear and being led by the things of God. Make sure that the decision that you have made is upward and not downward. Meaning that you made your decision based on what the Holy Spirit gave you. As we are drawing closer to the end of this 52 Week declaration and inspirational journey, you may notice that you have found yourself closer to God. If you have done what was encouraged so far, you can hear God's voice more clearly, because of the time you have spent with Him. This week decide what you will do regarding the decision you need to make. There is something else you have been procrastinating in doing. God says, make *up* your mind to do it now.

Jeremiah 33:3 {ESV} *Call to me and I will answer you, and will tell you great and hidden things that you have not known."*

What does it mean to you and how will you apply it this week?

Week 52:

*"When God's hand is on you,
no one can take it off!"*

You have made it this far, now remember; God is a Man of His word! If He said it, believe it! God is not like man. He keeps His promises no matter what outsiders say or think about you! Some may not think you deserve what God does. Truth is, you do not deserve His grace. You do not deserve His love, but by His mercy He extends it out to you regardless. His love reaches to you! The power of God will walk with you for the rest of your life. You shall new beginnings. This week you will decree and declare that divine abundance will be yours. Quite the noise and speak over your life this week, to not forget what God has promised you. You will have a Long-favored life. Just know that when you are favored, you will be hated by some. Remember that the hand of God is on you because you have trusted God with your life. He has favored you for believing in Him. Even when things are unexplainable, know that God is making up for everything that you have lost. There shall be nothing broken, missing, or lacking in your life. Praise God for keeping His hand on your life even when others did not approve. Be glad that He is not like man. Your blessings are not predicated on the likes of others. Your miracles are on the way! This week will be different. Claim it! You shall have what you say!

<u>1 Corinthians 10:13</u> {KJV} *There hath no temptation taken you but such as is common to man: but God is faithful, who will not suffer you to be tempted above that ye are able; but will with the temptation also make a way to escape, that ye may be able to bear it.*

What does it mean to you and how will you apply it this week?

The Conclusion of The Matter

Proverbs 1:7 *{KJV} The fear of the LORD is the beginning of knowledge: but fools despise wisdom and instruction.*

My prayer is that your walk with our Father (GOD) has been strengthened by the quotes of my earthly father, the late honorable Bishop E. Floyd, Jr. and mother, Prophetess Armatha Floyd, along with the aspirations and declarations that were given to me by the Holy Spirit. God is truly the source of our strength.

Understanding the sovereignty of God demands that a sinful humanity must repent by asking God for forgiveness and He is willing to forgive. There is nothing too difficult for our (Father) God. May you walk in the faith and believe in the life, death, and resurrection "for man's sin" by the shed blood of Jesus the Christ, the Son of God. John 3:16 KJV: *For God so loved the world, that he gave his only begotten Son, that whosoever believeth in him should not perish, but have everlasting life.* "Everyone will see His face but not everyone will stay with Him."- Prophetess Armatha Floyd My prayer is that our stay is with God for eternity.

Lastly, if you have not already, accept Jesus as your personal Savior and join a local body of believers. In my honorable father's words, "If you don't have a church home already, search for a Bible Based Church." Do not think for a moment that you will ever find a church that will not have some type of shortage. After all, there was a church in the Bible, called 'Corinth' that had a LOVE shortage. Therefore, allow the Holy Spirit to lead you to a church and let the church get in you."

In my Heavenly Father's Will, Mega Blessings!

Waticia Floyd McDonald

Read and enjoy the scriptures that were inspired from,

When Wisdom Speaks, Knowledge Listens:

James 1:5 ESV

If any of you lacks wisdom, let him ask God, who gives generously to all without reproach, and it will be given him.

Proverbs 1:7 ESV

The fear of the Lord is the beginning of knowledge; fools despise wisdom and instruction.

Psalm 111:10 ESV

The fear of the Lord is the beginning of wisdom; all those who practice it have a good understanding. His praise endures forever!

Proverbs 2:1-22 ESV

My son, if you receive my words and treasure up my commandments with you, making your ear attentive to wisdom and inclining your heart to understanding; yes, if you call out for insight and raise your voice for understanding, if you seek it like silver and search for it as for hidden treasures, then you will understand the fear of the Lord and find the knowledge of God.

Ecclesiastes 7:12 ESV

For the protection of wisdom is like the protection of money, and the advantage of knowledge is that wisdom preserves the life of him who has it.

Isaiah 11:2 ESV

And the Spirit of the Lord shall rest upon him, the Spirit of wisdom and understanding, the Spirit of counsel and might, the Spirit of knowledge and the fear of the Lord.

Colossians 2:8 ESV

See to it that no one takes you captive by philosophy and empty deceit, according to human tradition, according to the elemental spirits of the world, and not according to Christ.

1 Timothy 2:4 ESV

Who desires all people to be saved and to come to the knowledge of the truth?

Matthew 7:7-8 ESV

Ask, and it will be given to you; seek, and you will find; knock, and it will be opened to you. For everyone who asks receives, and the one who seeks finds, and to the one who knocks it will be opened.

1 Corinthians 3:19-20 ESV

For the wisdom of this world is folly with God. For it is written, "He catches the wise in their craftiness," and again, "The Lord knows the thoughts of the wise, that they are futile."

James 3:17 ESV

But the wisdom from above is first pure, then peaceable, gentle, open to reason, full of mercy and good fruits, impartial and sincere.

Proverbs 4:1-27 ESV

Hear, O sons, a father's instruction, and be attentive, that you may gain insight, for I give you good precepts; do not forsake my teaching. When I was a son with my father, tender, the only one in the sight of my mother, he taught me and said to me, "Let your heart hold fast my words; keep my commandments, and live. Get wisdom; get insight; do not forget, and do not turn away from the words of my mouth."

Proverbs 2:6 ESV

For the Lord gives wisdom; from his mouth come knowledge and understanding.

2 Chronicles 1:7-12 ESV

In that night God appeared to Solomon, and said to him, "Ask what I shall give you." And Solomon said to God, "You have shown great and steadfast love to David my father, and have made me king in his place. O Lord God, let your word to David my father be now fulfilled, for you have made me king over a people as numerous as the dust of the earth. Give me now wisdom and knowledge to go out and come in before this people, for who can govern this people of yours, which is so great?" God answered Solomon, "Because this was in your heart, and you have not asked possessions, wealth, honor, or the life of those who hate you, and have not even asked long life, but have asked wisdom and knowledge for yourself that you may govern my people over whom I have made you king."

James 3:15-18 ESV

This is not the wisdom that comes down from above, but is earthly, unspiritual, demonic. For where jealousy and selfish ambition exist, there will be disorder and every vile practice. But the wisdom from above is first pure, then peaceable, gentle, open to reason, full of mercy and good fruits, impartial and sincere. And a harvest of righteousness is sown in peace by those who make peace.

Romans 1:22-25 ESV

Claiming to be wise, they became fools, and exchanged the glory of the immortal God for images resembling mortal man and birds and animals and creeping things. Therefore God gave them up in the lusts of their hearts to impurity, to the dishonoring of their bodies among themselves, because they exchanged the truth about God for a lie and worshiped and served the creature rather than the Creator, who is blessed forever! Amen.

Proverbs 20:15 ESV

There is gold and abundance of costly stones, but the lips of knowledge are a precious jewel.

Psalm 91:1-16 ESV

He who dwells in the shelter of the Most High will abide in the shadow of the Almighty. I will say to the Lord, "My refuge and my fortress, my God, in whom I trust." For he will deliver you from the snare of the fowler and from the deadly pestilence. He will cover you with his pinions, and under his wings you will find refuge; his faithfulness is a shield and buckler. You will not fear the terror of the night, nor the arrow that flies by day.

Proverbs 2:3-7 ESV Yes, if you call out for insight and raise your voice for understanding, if you seek it like silver and search for it as for hidden treasures, then you will understand the fear of the Lord and find the knowledge of God. For the Lord gives wisdom; from his mouth come knowledge and understanding; he stores up sound wisdom for the upright; he is a shield to those who walk in integrity.

1 Corinthians 1:20 ESV

Where is the one who is wise? Where is the scribe? Where is the debater of this age? Has not God made foolish the wisdom of the world?

Proverbs 16:16 ESV

How much better to get wisdom than gold! To get understanding is to be chosen rather than silver.

Proverbs 11:2 ESV

When pride comes, then comes disgrace, but with the humble is wisdom.

Proverbs 13:4 ESV

The soul of the sluggard craves and gets nothing, while the soul of the diligent is richly supplied.

Proverbs 9:10 ESV

The fear of the Lord is the beginning of wisdom, and the knowledge of the Holy One is insight.

James 3:13 ESV

Who is wise and understanding among you? By his good conduct let him show his works in the meekness of wisdom.

Psalm 90:12 ESV

So teach us to number our days that we may get a heart of wisdom.

1 Corinthians 1:30 ESV

And because of him you are in Christ Jesus, who became to us wisdom from God, righteousness and sanctification and redemption,

Proverbs 18:2-5 ESV

A fool takes no pleasure in understanding, but only in expressing his opinion. When wickedness comes, contempt comes also, and with dishonor comes disgrace. The words of a man's mouth are deep waters; the fountain of wisdom is a bubbling brook. It is not good to be partial to the wicked or to deprive the righteous of justice.

Daniel 2:23 ESV

To you, O God of my fathers, I give thanks and praise, for you have given me wisdom and might, and have now made known to me what we asked of you, for you have made known to us the king's matter.

Proverbs 18:15 ESV

An intelligent heart acquires knowledge, and the ear of the wise seeks knowledge.

Proverbs 13:10 ESV

By insolence comes nothing but strife, but with those who take advice is wisdom.

Proverbs 3:7 ESV

Be not wise in your own eyes; fear the Lord, and turn away from evil.

1 Corinthians 1:18-29 ESV

For the word of the cross is folly to those who are perishing, but to us who are being saved it is the power of God. For it is written, "I will destroy the wisdom of the wise, and the discernment of the discerning I will thwart." Where is the one who is wise? Where is the scribe? Where is the debater of this age? Has not God made foolish the wisdom of the world? For since, in the wisdom of God, the world did not know God through wisdom, it pleased God through the folly of what we preach to save those who believe. For Jews demand signs and Greeks seek wisdom.

Proverbs 15:33 ESV

The fear of the Lord is instruction in wisdom, and humility comes before honor.

Job 28:28 ESV

And he said to man, 'Behold, the fear of the Lord, that is wisdom, and to turn away from evil is understanding.'

Job 12:12 ESV

Wisdom is with the aged, and understanding in length of days.

John 3:16-17 ESV

For God so loved the world, that he gave his only Son, that whoever believes in him should not perish but have eternal life. For God did not send his Son into the world to condemn the world, but in order that the world might be saved through him.

Isaiah 40:28 ESV

Have you not known? Have you not heard? The Lord is the everlasting God, the Creator of the ends of the earth. He does not faint or grow weary; his understanding is unsearchable.

Psalm 119:97-98 ESV

Oh how I love your law! It is my meditation all the day. Your commandment makes me wiser than my enemies, for it is ever with me.

Proverbs 19:8 ESV

Whoever gets sense loves his own soul; he who keeps understanding will discover good.

1 John 4:18 ESV

There is no fear in love, but perfect love casts out fear. For fear has to do with punishment, and whoever fears has not been perfected in love.

Romans 11:33 ESV

Oh, the depth of the riches and wisdom and knowledge of God! How unsearchable are his judgments and how inscrutable his ways!

Proverbs 15:30-33 ESV

The light of the eyes rejoices the heart, and good news refreshes the bones. The ear that listens to life-giving reproof will dwell among the wise. Whoever ignores instruction despises himself, but he who listens to reproof gains intelligence. The fear of the Lord is instruction in wisdom, and humility comes before honor.

Colossians 2:2-3 ESV

That their hearts may be encouraged, being knit together in love, to reach all the riches of full assurance of understanding and the knowledge of God's mystery, which is Christ, in whom are hidden all the treasures of wisdom and knowledge.

Proverbs 14:8 ESV

The wisdom of the prudent is to discern his way, but the folly of fools is deceiving.

Daniel 2:19-23 ESV

Then the mystery was revealed to Daniel in a vision of the night. Then Daniel blessed the God of heaven. Daniel answered and said: "Blessed be the name of God forever and ever, to whom belong wisdom and might. He changes times and seasons; he removes kings and sets up kings; he gives wisdom to the wise and knowledge to those who have understanding; he reveals deep and hidden things; he knows what is in the darkness, and the light dwells with him. To you, O God of my fathers, I give thanks and praise, for you have given me wisdom and might, and have now made known to me what we asked of you, for you have made known to us the king's matter."

Proverbs 10:8 ESV

The wise of heart will receive commandments, but a babbling fool will come to ruin.

Colossians 1:9 ESV

And so, from the day we heard, we have not ceased to pray for you, asking that you may be filled with the knowledge of his will in all spiritual wisdom and understanding.

1 Corinthians 3:18 ESV

Let no one deceive himself. If anyone among you thinks that he is wise in this age, let him become a fool that he may become wise.

Proverbs 19:20 ESV

Listen to advice and accept instruction, that you may gain wisdom in the future.

Proverbs 4:26-27 ESV

Ponder the path of your feet; then all your ways will be sure. Do not swerve to the right or to the left; turn your foot away from evil.

Matthew 7:24 ESV

Everyone then who hears these words of mine and does them will be like a wise man who built his house on the rock.

1 Corinthians 1:27-31 ESV

But God chose what is foolish in the world to shame the wise; God chose what is weak in the world to shame the strong; God chose what is low and despised in the world, even things that are not, to bring to nothing things that are, so that no human being might boast in the presence of God. And because of him you are in Christ Jesus, who became to us wisdom from God, righteousness and sanctification and redemption, so that, as it is written, "Let the one who boasts, boast in the Lord."

Proverbs 29:11 ESV

A fool gives full vent to his spirit, but a wise man quietly holds it back.

Proverbs 18:2 ESV

A fool takes no pleasure in understanding, but only in expressing his opinion.

Ephesians 5:15-16 ESV

Look carefully then how you walk, not as unwise but as wise, making the best use of the time, because the days are evil.

1 Corinthians 1:19-23 ESV

For it is written, "I will destroy the wisdom of the wise, and the discernment of the discerning I will thwart." Where is the one who is wise? Where is the scribe? Where is the debater of this age? Has not God made foolish the wisdom of the world? For since, in the wisdom of God, the world did not know God through wisdom, it pleased God through the folly of what we preach to save those who believe. For Jews demand signs and Greeks seek wisdom, but we preach Christ crucified, a stumbling block to Jews and folly to Gentiles.

Isaiah 28:29 ESV

This also comes from the Lord of hosts; he is wonderful in counsel and excellent in wisdom.

Jude 1:24-25 ESV

Now to him who is able to keep you from stumbling and to present you blameless before the presence of his glory with great joy, to the only God, our Savior, through Jesus Christ our Lord, be glory, majesty, dominion, and authority, before all time and now and forever. Amen.

Colossians 4:5-6 ESV

Walk in wisdom toward outsiders, making the best use of the time. Let your speech always be gracious, seasoned with salt, so that you may know how you ought to answer each person.

1 Corinthians 1:25 ESV

For the foolishness of God is wiser than men, and the weakness of God is stronger than men.

Daniel 2:21 ESV

He changes times and seasons; he removes kings and sets up kings; he gives wisdom to the wise and knowledge to those who have understanding.

Ecclesiastes 2:26 ESV

For to the one who pleases him God has given wisdom and knowledge and joy, but to the sinner he has given the business of gathering and collecting, only to give to one who pleases God. This also is vanity and a striving after wind.

Proverbs 14:29 ESV

Whoever is slow to anger has great understanding, but he who has a hasty temper exalts folly.

Luke 21:15 ESV

For I will give you a mouth and wisdom, which none of your adversaries will be able to withstand or contradict.

Jeremiah 51:15-16 ESV

It is he who made the earth by his power, who established the world by his wisdom, and by his understanding stretched out the heavens. When he utters his voice there is a tumult of waters in the heavens, and he makes the mist rise from the ends of the earth. He makes lightning for the rain, and he brings forth the wind from his storehouses.

Jeremiah 10:12-13 ESV

It is he who made the earth by his power, who established the world by his wisdom, and by his understanding stretched out the heavens. When he utters his voice, there is a tumult of waters in the heavens, and he makes the mist rise from the ends of the earth. He makes lightning for the rain, and he brings forth the wind from his storehouses.

Isaiah 53:6-10 ESV

All we like sheep have gone astray; we have turned—every one—to his own way; and the Lord has laid on him the iniquity of us all. He was oppressed, and he was afflicted, yet he opened not his mouth; like a lamb that is led to the slaughter, and like a sheep that before its shearers is silent, so he opened not his mouth. By oppression and judgment he was taken away; and as for his generation, who considered that he was cut off out of the land of the living, stricken for the transgression of my people? And they made his grave with the wicked and with a rich man in his death, although he had done no violence, and there was no deceit in his mouth. Yet it was the will of the Lord to crush him; he has put him to grief; when his soul makes an offering for guilt, he shall see his offspring; he shall prolong his days; the will of the Lord shall prosper in his hand.

Isaiah 33:6 ESV

And he will be the stability of your times, abundance of salvation, wisdom, and knowledge; the fear of the Lord is Zion's treasure.

Proverbs 29:15 ESV

The rod and reproof give wisdom, but a child left to himself brings shame to his mother.

Psalm 37:30 ESV

The mouth of the righteous utters wisdom, and his tongue speaks justice.

1 Peter 5:5-9 ESV

Likewise, you who are younger, be subject to the elders. Clothe yourselves, all of you, with humility toward one another, for "God opposes the proud but gives grace to the humble." Humble yourselves, therefore, under the mighty hand of God so that at the proper time he may exalt you, casting all your anxieties on him, because he cares for you. Be sober-minded; be watchful. Your adversary the devil prowls around like a roaring lion, seeking someone to devour. Resist him, firm in your faith, knowing that the same kinds of suffering are being experienced by your brotherhood throughout the world.

Special Tribute

Here's to the wisest man I've ever known, Bishop E. Floyd, Jr.!

Dad, your legacy will live on forever. The world is better because of you. God certainly outdid himself when he made you. We are forever grateful for your love, protection and guidance to so many around the world. Dad, I've had to share you with people all of my life and I'll keep sharing, because someone needs this same wisdom and love you passed on for generations.

My father pastored for 55 years before he transitioned to Glory. My mother is now carrying on the torch, and with the help of God is doing an outstanding job.

To God be the Glory! I will continue to assist my mother in ministry and although we all miss Dad, we all know that the Kingdom of God is in us and the vision must go on.

Please enjoy other phrases you may be familiar with from past generations. Add to the list from your loved ones. "When Wisdom Speaks, Knowledge Listens"

Other friendly phrases from Mother's and Father's Diary continued but not mentioned:

That's Ms. Emma
I remember the time water was free
Time is free but far spent
I don't mean no harm...
Have her take off her shoes and see if her feet don't look like mine. I'm the husband, something better look like me.
The "I am" sent me, and you can't send me back
You are some kind of friend
Today's music and food had nothing on our day
Zap
Time is too slow for those who wait, too swift for those who fear, too long for those who grieve, too short for those who rejoice, but for those who love, time is eternity
I heard that
Don't trade today for tomorrow
I am as full as a tick
They won't work in a pie factory
I shot my goat
Alright Fellows...
Don't hang around people that know something about every topic you bring up
Well Hello Lights...
I Beg your Pardon...
Are you mothers praying for me over there?...
Hit it Fellows!...
I'm just going to tell the Truth!...
You got to pray; y'all ain't praying...
Let me sing my song, Jesus, Jesus...
My Buddy

Sit so you can watch as well as pray for your husband…
Well Sir!…
It takes a long time to grow an old friend
It's coming to a "Ba-loo-shaa"….

Proverbs 29:3 {NET} *He who loves wisdom makes his father glad, but a companion of prostitutes squanders his wealth.*

www.ingramcontent.com/pod-product-compliance
Ingram Content Group UK Ltd.
Pitfield, Milton Keynes, MK11 3LW, UK
UKHW022221230426
12048UKWH00016BA/989